FAMOUS
ATHLETES

# STEPHEN CURRY

by Mari Schuh

Pebble®
Plus

CAPSTONE PRESS
a capstone imprint

Pebble Plus is published by Capstone Press,
1710 Roe Crest Drive, North Mankato, Minnesota 56003
www.capstonepub.com

**Library of Congress Cataloging-in-Publication Data**
Stephen Curry / by Mari Schuh.
     pages cm. — (Pebble Plus. Famous Athletes)
  Includes webography.
  Includes bibliographical references and index.
  Summary: "Presents the life of professional basketball athlete Stephen Curry in an
introductory biography with a timeline and photos"— Provided by publisher.
  ISBN 978-1-4914-8509-5 (library binding)
  ISBN 978-1-4914-8529-3 (paperback)
  ISBN 978-1-4914-8525-5 (eBook PDF)
  1. Curry, Stephen, 1988-—Juvenile literature. 2. Basketball players—United States—
Biography—Juvenile literature. I. Title.
  GV884.C88S38 2016
  796.323092—dc23
  [B]                                              2015021136

**Editorial Credits**
Gina Kammer, editor; Juliette Peters, designer; Eric Gohl, media researcher;
Lori Barbeau, production specialist

**Photo Credits**
Getty Images: NBAE/Andrew D. Bernstein, 5, NBAE/Don Smith, 15, NBAE/Tim Cattera, 7;
Lila J & Arnold W Photography: 9; Newscom: Cal Sport Media/Albert Pena, cover, Cal Sport
Media/John Green, 1, 17, EPA/Larry W. Smith, 21, Icon SMI/David Allio, 13, MCT/David T.
Foster III, 11, USA Today Sports/Derick E. Hingle, 19

Design Elements: Shutterstock

## Note to Parents and Teachers

The Famous Athletes set supports national curriculum standards for social studies
related to people, places, and culture. This book describes and illustrates Stephen
Curry. The images support early readers in understanding the text. The repetition of
words and phrases helps early readers learn new words. This book also introduces
early readers to subject-specific vocabulary words, which are defined in the Glossary
section. Early readers may need assistance to read some words and to use the Table of
Contents, Glossary, Read More, Internet Sites, Critical Thinking Using the Common
Core, and Index sections of the book.

Printed in the United States of America in North Mankato, Minnesota.
052016   009780R

# TABLE OF CONTENTS

# EARLY LIFE

Basketball star Stephen Curry
was born March 14, 1988.
He grew up watching and playing
basketball. His dad played in the NBA.
Stephen watched his dad's games.

NBA stands for National
Basketball Association.

born in
Akron, Ohio

Stephen grew up in Charlotte,

North Carolina. He played

basketball with his brother Seth.

They played in their backyard. They

played for hours.

1988
born in
Akron, Ohio

6

Stephen (right) talks with his brother, Seth (left), after his brother's game.

Stephen was a star player in high school.

He led the basketball team to three conference titles.

The team also played in the state playoffs.

Stephen earned all-conference and

all-state honors in 2005 and 2006.

1988
born in
Akron, Ohio

2005
2006
earns all-
conference and
all-state honors
as a junior
and senior

# COLLEGE YEARS

After high school Stephen went to Davidson College in North Carolina. In 2008 he led his team to victories in the NCAA Tournament. He was named to All-American teams in 2008 and 2009.

NCAA stands for National Collegiate Athletic Association.

**1988**

born in Akron, Ohio

**2005 2006**

earns all-conference and all-state honors as a junior and senior

**2008**

leads Davidson Wildcats to victories in the NCAA Tournament

11

Stephen was one of the best shooters in college basketball. He led the nation in scoring for the 2008-2009 season. He scored an average of 28.6 points a game.

**1988**

born in Akron, Ohio

**2005 2006**

earns all-conference and all-state honors as a junior and senior

**2008**

leads Davidson Wildcats to victories in the NCAA Tournament

**2008-2009**

becomes top college scorer

# NBA STAR

In 2009 Stephen started playing in the NBA. He played well his first season. Stephen scored an average of 17.5 points a game. He was runner-up for the Rookie of the Year Award.

**1988**

born in Akron, Ohio

**2005 2006**

earns all-conference and all-state honors as a junior and senior

**2008**

leads Davidson Wildcats to victories in the NCAA Tournament

**2008- 2009**

becomes top college scorer

**2009**

starts to play for the NBA's Golden State Warriors

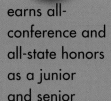

Stephen earned more awards.

In 2011 he won the

NBA Sportsmanship Award.

It is given to a player who plays fair

and respects others.

**1988**
born in
Akron, Ohio

**2005 2006**
earns all-
conference and
all-state honors
as a junior
and senior

**2008**
leads Davidson
Wildcats to
victories in the
NCAA
Tournament

**2008– 2009**
becomes top
college
scorer

**2009**
starts to play
for the NBA's
Golden State
Warriors

**2011**
wins NBA
Sportsmanship
Award

Stephen is one of the NBA's best shooters.

He led the NBA in three-point goals

for three seasons in a row.

He has also played in the

All-Star Game two times.

**1988**

born in
Akron, Ohio

**2005 2006**

earns all-
conference and
all-state honors
as a junior
and senior

**2008**

leads Davidson
Wildcats to
victories in the
NCAA
Tournament

**2008– 2009**

becomes top
college
scorer

**2009**

starts to play
for the NBA's
Golden State
Warriors

**2011**

wins NBA
Sportsmanship
Award

Stephen was named Most Valuable Player

for the 2014-2015 season.

He also helped his team win the

NBA championship in 2015. Stephen

wants to win many more games.

**1988**

born in
Akron, Ohio

**2005-2006**

earns all-
conference and
all-state honors
as a junior
and senior

**2008**

leads Davidson
Wildcats to
victories in the
NCAA
Tournament

**2008-2009**

becomes top
college
scorer

**2009**

starts to play
for the NBA's
Golden State
Warriors

**2011**

wins NBA
Sportsmanship
Award

**2015**

named MVP for
the 2014-2015
season

Stephen (front, second from right) celebrates the NBA championship with his team.

# GLOSSARY

**All-Star Game**—a special game played every year in which the best NBA players play against each other

**average**—a number found by adding all scores together and dividing by the number of scores

**championship**—a contest or tournament that decides which team is the best

**conference**—a group of basketball teams from different universities that play against one another

**NBA**—National Basketball Association

**NCAA**—the National Collegiate Athletic Association, which runs college basketball

**playoffs**—a series of games played after the regular season to decide a championship

**respect**—to treat others in a polite and honest way

**rookie**—a player who is playing his or her first year on a team

**runner-up**—a player that takes second place

**season**—a time of the year; the NBA's regular season starts in the fall and ends in the spring.

**title**—an award given to the winner of a tournament

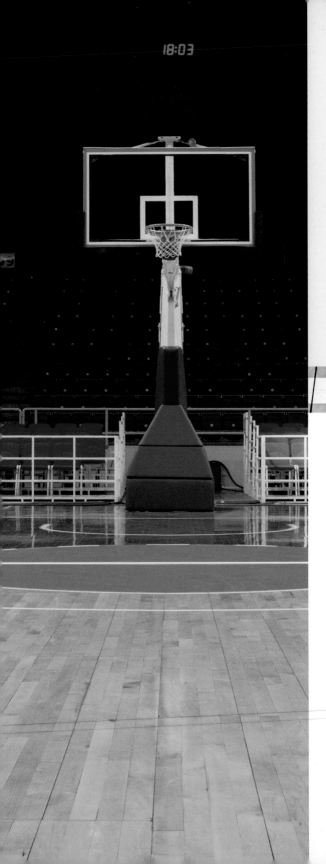

# READ MORE

**Doeden, Matt**. *All About Basketball*. North Mankato, Minn.: Capstone Press, 2015.

**Lindeen, Mary**. *Let's Play Basketball!* Chicago: Norwood House Press, 2015.

**Nagelhout, Ryan**. *I Love Basketball.* New York: Gareth Stevens Publishing, 2015.

**Nelson, Robin**. *Basketball is Fun*! Minneapolis, Minn.: Lerner Publications, 2014.

# INTERNET SITES

FactHound offers a safe, fun way to find Internet sites related to this book. All of the sites on FactHound have been researched by our staff.

Here's all you do:

Visit *www.facthound.com*

Type in this code: 9781491485095

 **Super-cool stuff!** Check out projects, games and lots more at **www.capstonekids.com**

# CRITICAL THINKING
# USING THE COMMON CORE

1. How did Stephen's childhood help him become a basketball star? (Key Ideas and Details)

2. Stephen won the NBA Sportsmanship Award in 2011. How did he behave to get this award? Why is this award important? (Integration of Knowledge and Ideas)

# INDEX